THIS BOOK
BELONGS TO:

_____

APPLE

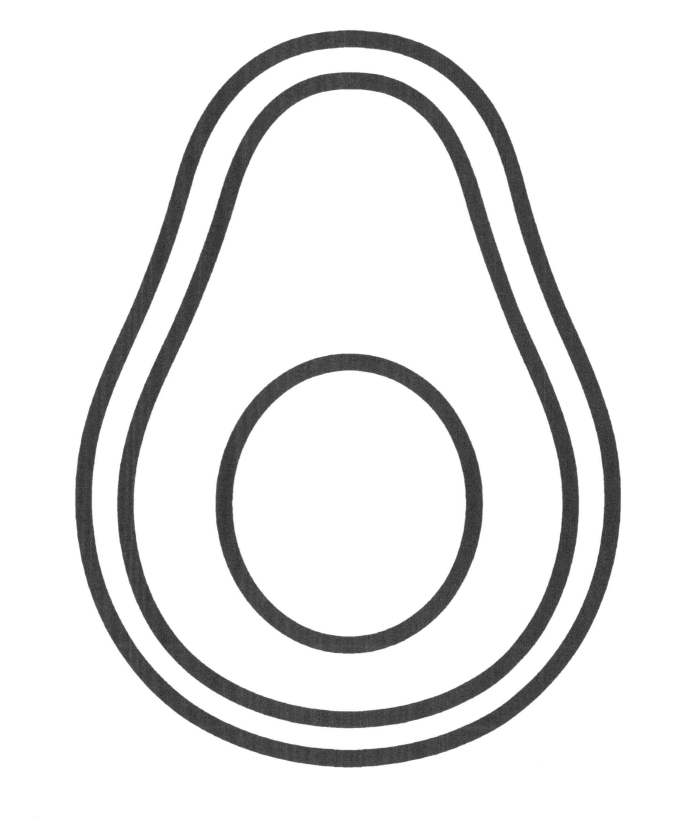

AVOCADO

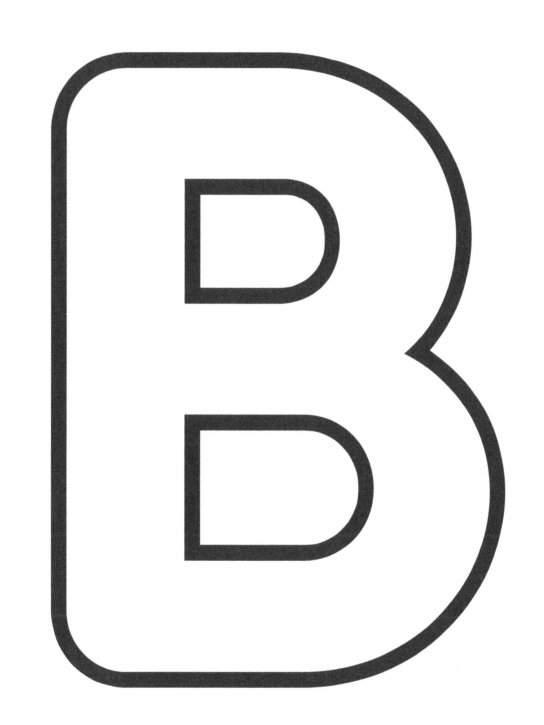

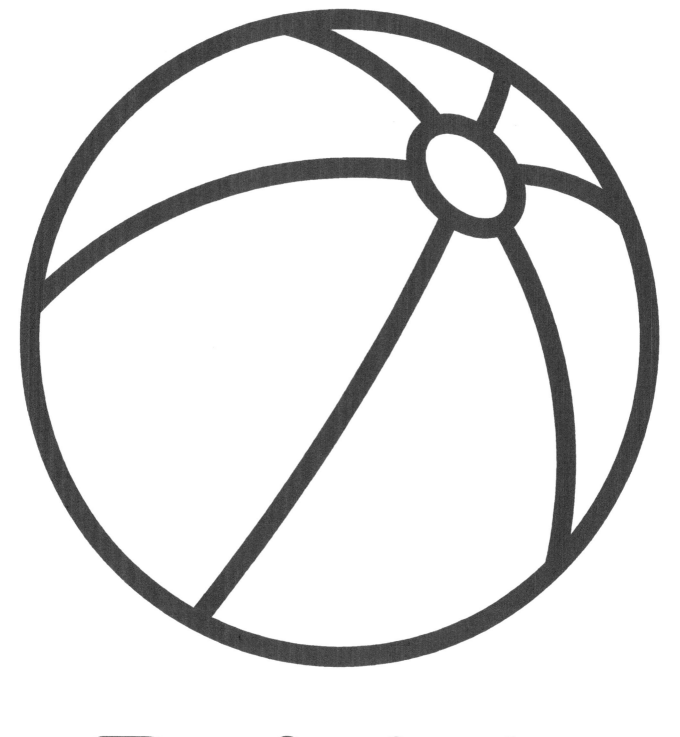

BALL

BEE

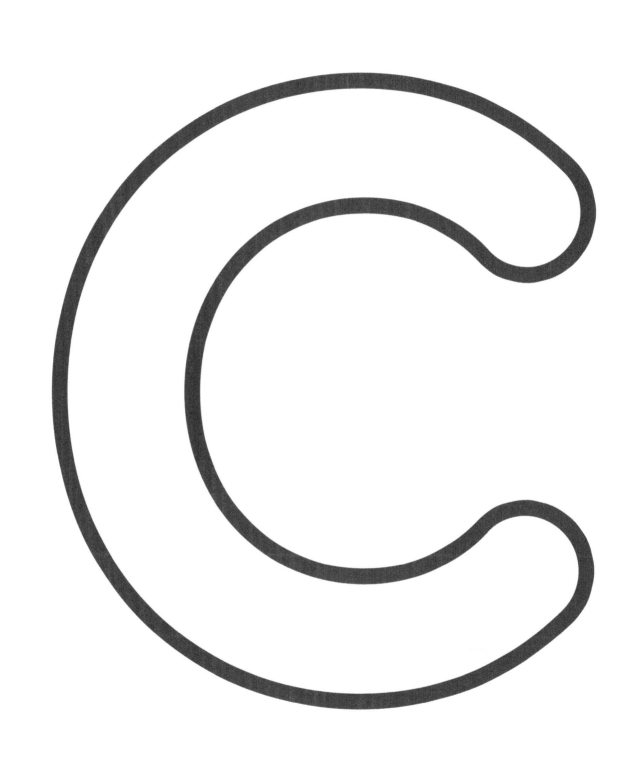

CACTUS

CRAYON

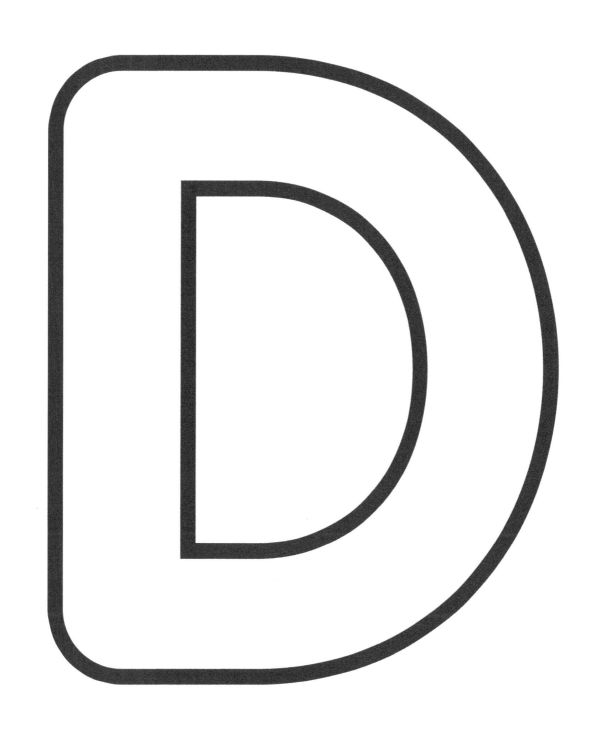

DIAMOND

DOG

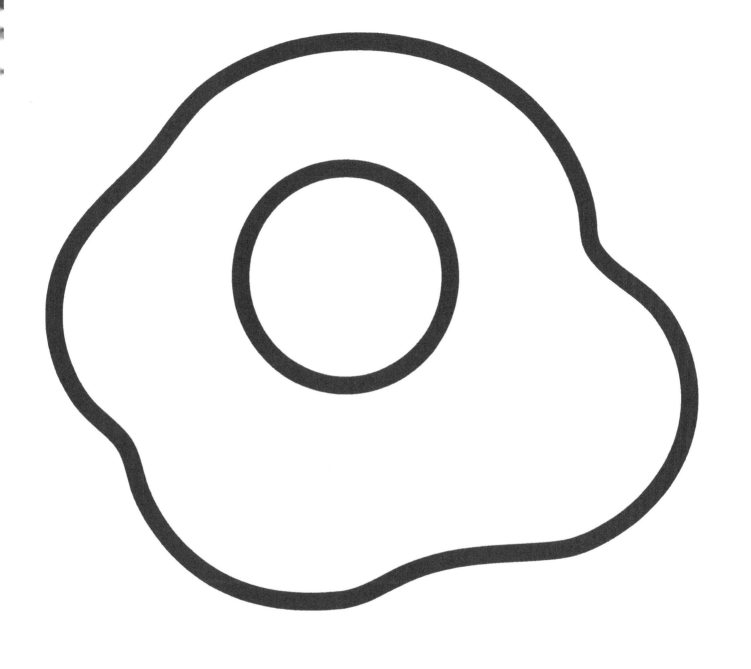

EGG

EGGPLANT

F

FROG

FOOTBALL

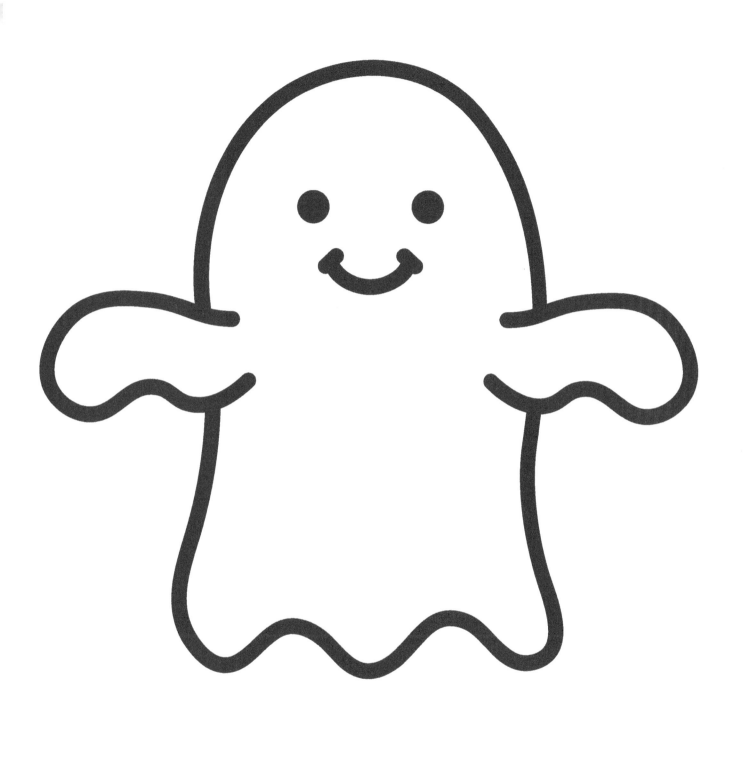

GHOST

GRAPES

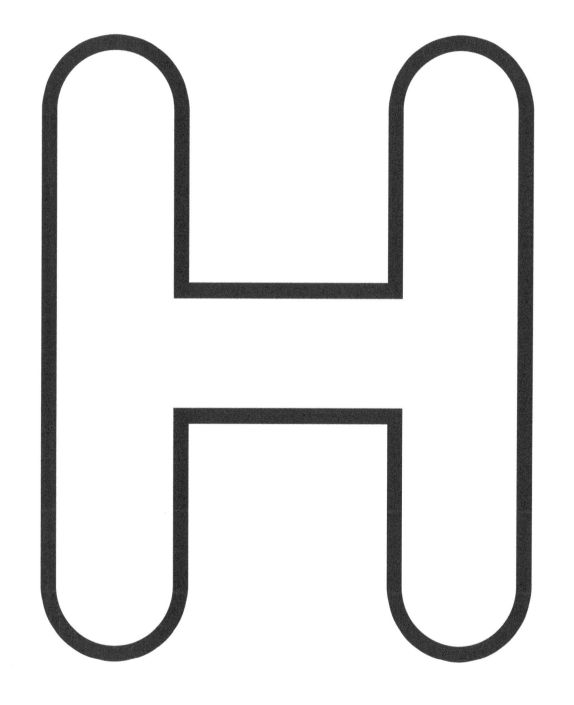

HORSE

HAMBURGER

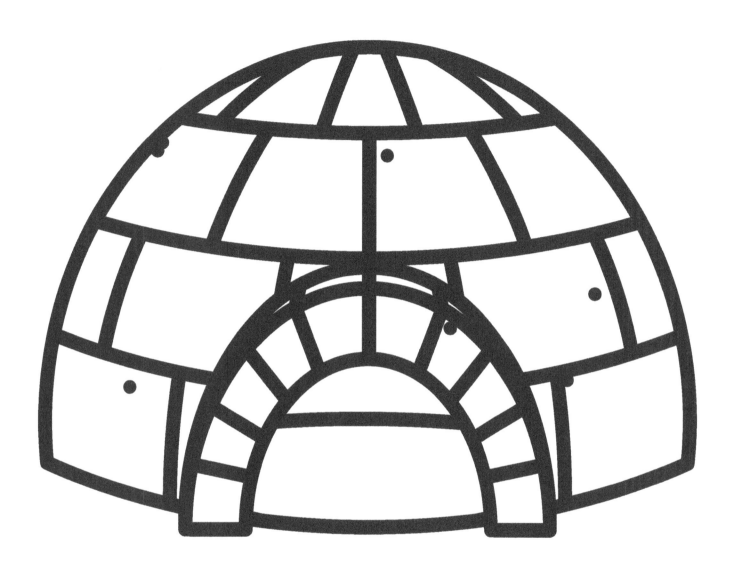

IGLOO

ISLAND

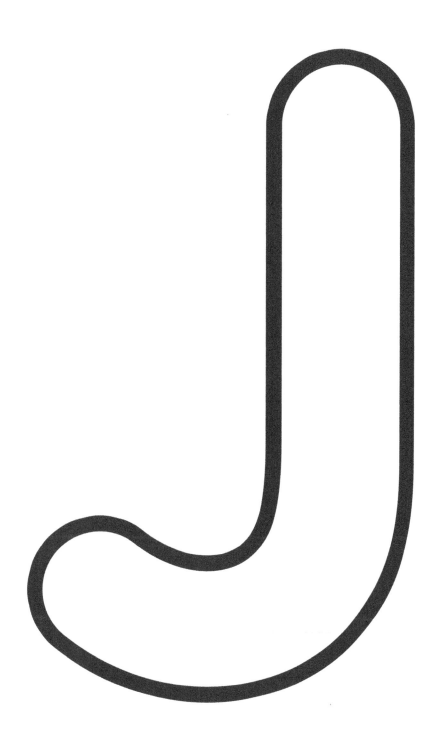

JELLY

JELLYFISH

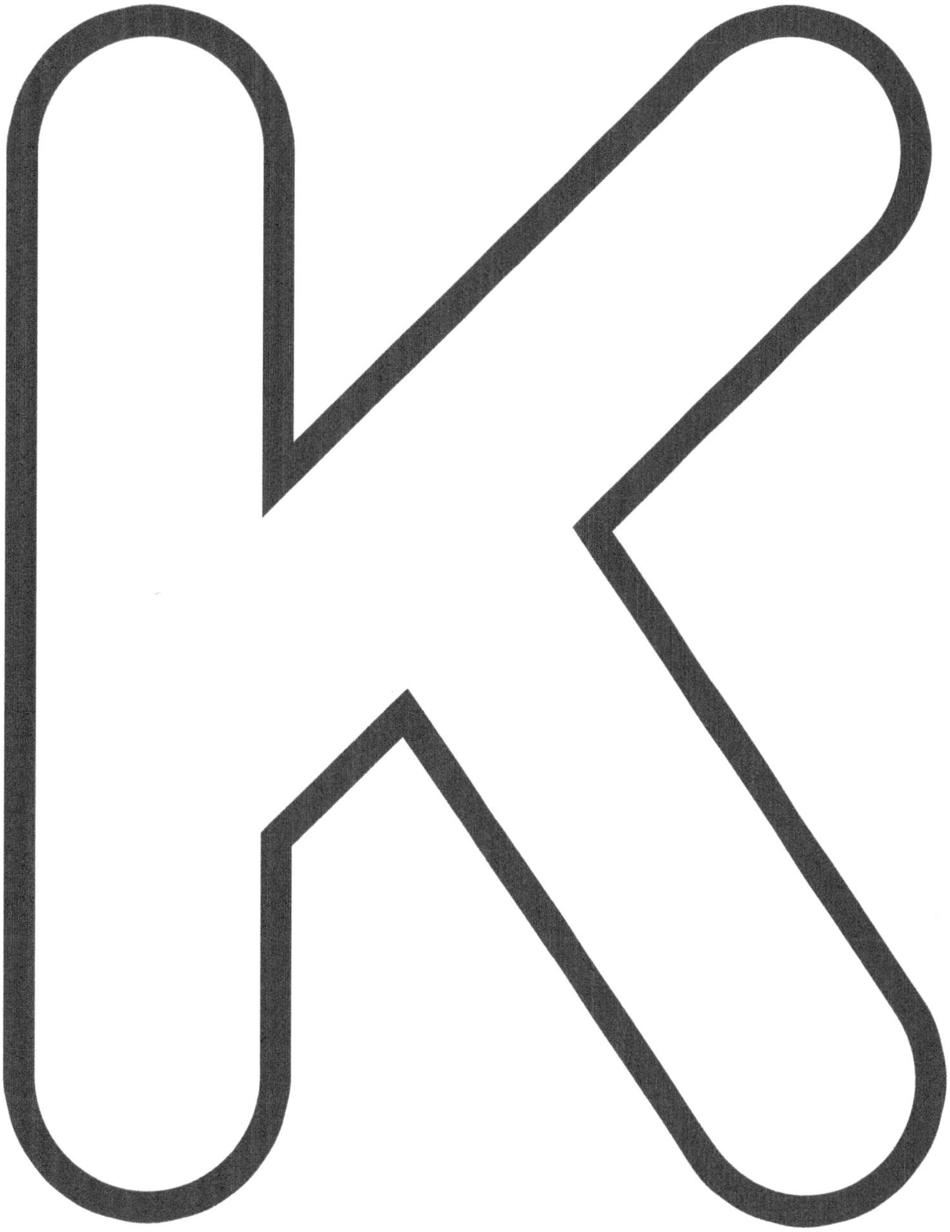
K

KETTLE

KOALA

LLAMA

LOLLIPOP

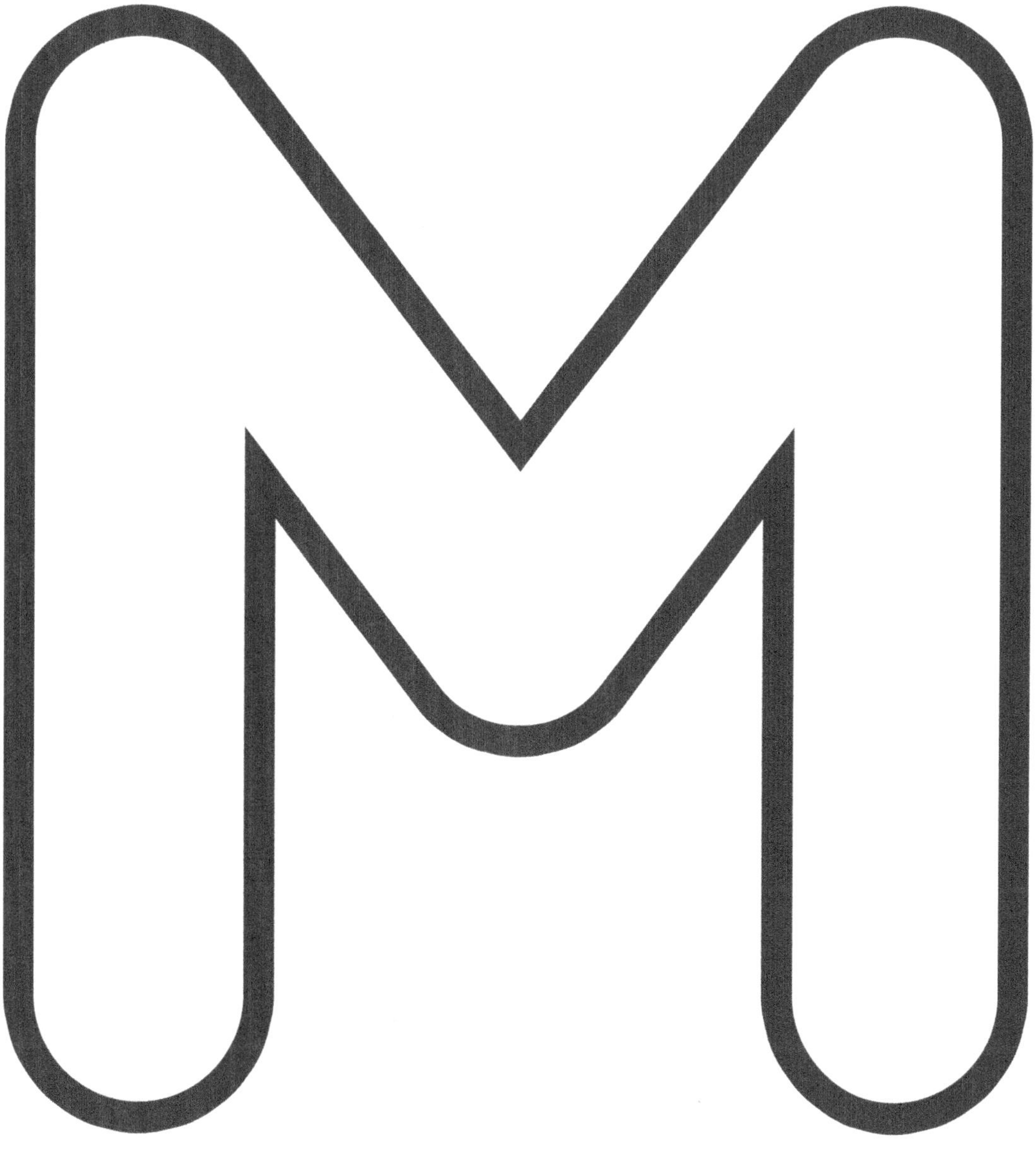
M

MUSHROOM

MOUSE

NOTEBOOK

NEST

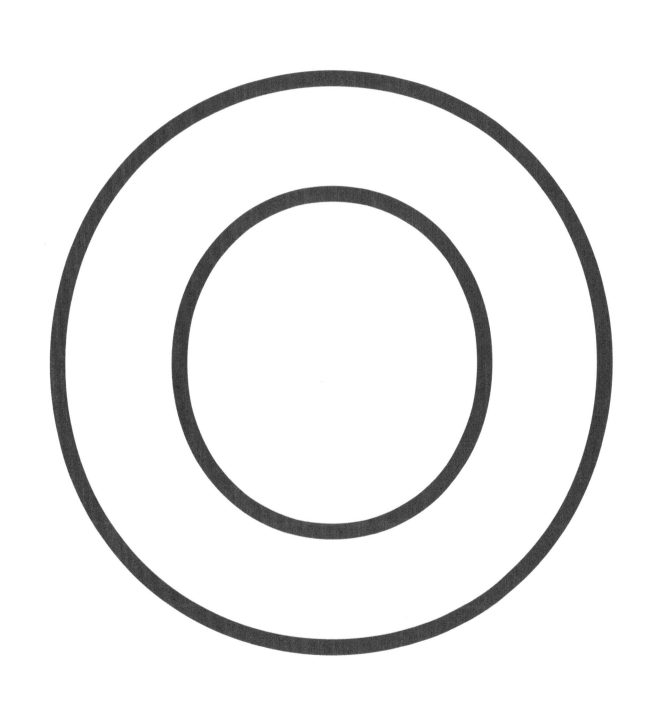

OX

OCTOPUS

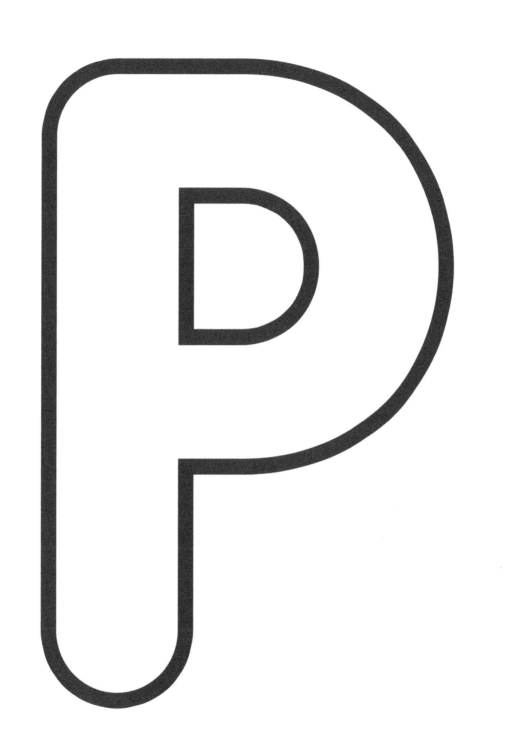

PANDA

POPCORN

QUARTER

QUAIL

RABBIT

ROCKET

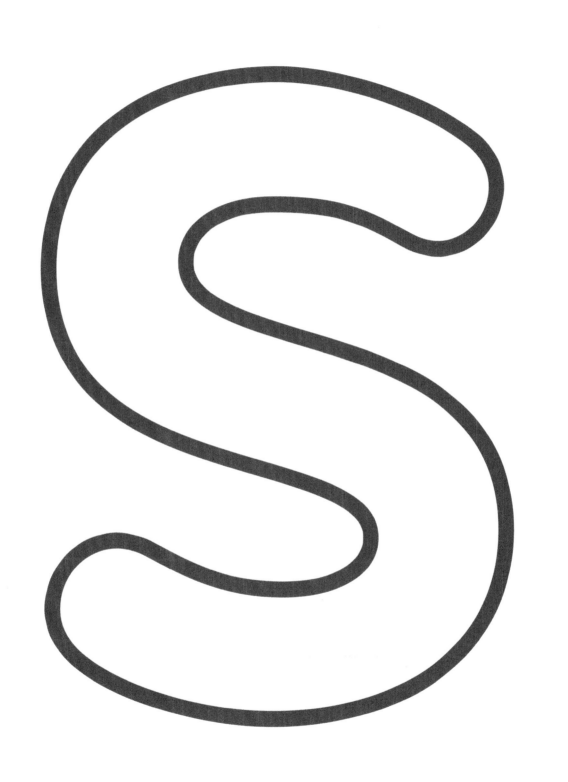

SHARK

SHELL

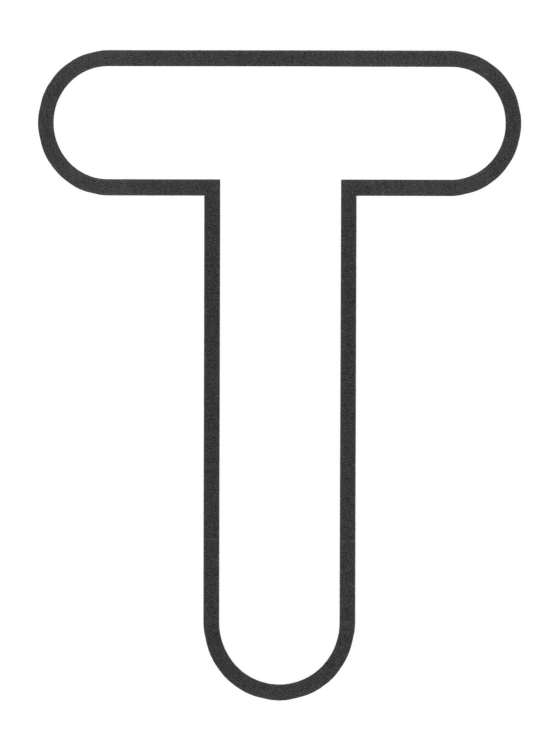

TREE

TRAIN

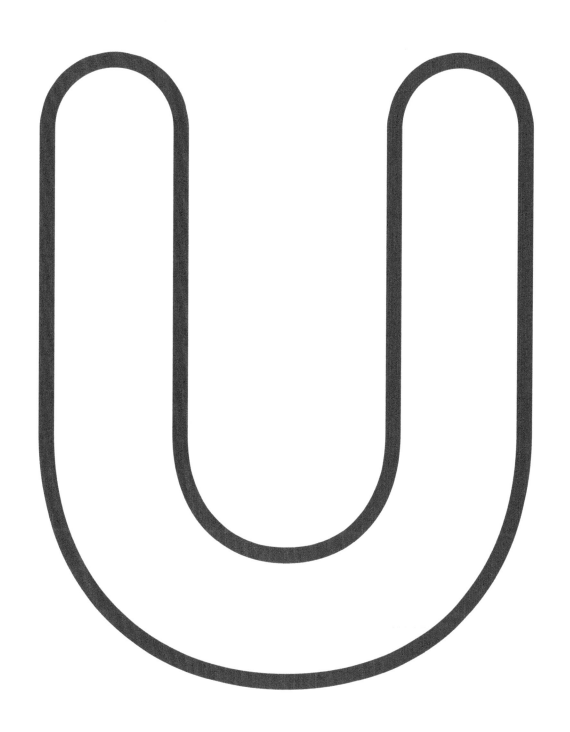

UMBRELLA

UNICORN

VASE

VOLCANO

WHALE

WOLF

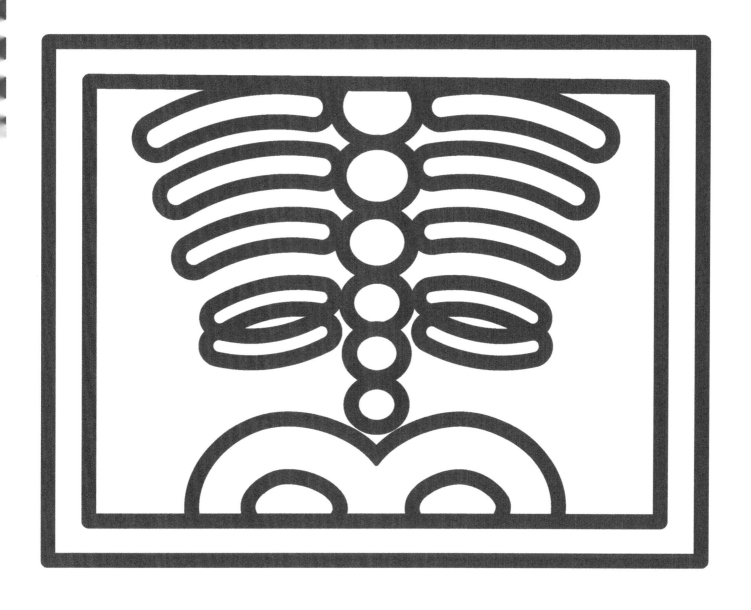

X-RAY

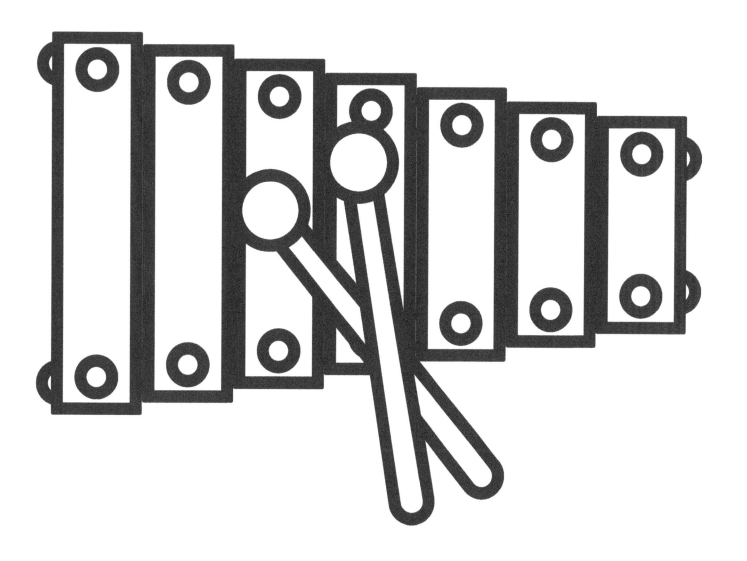

XYLOPHONE

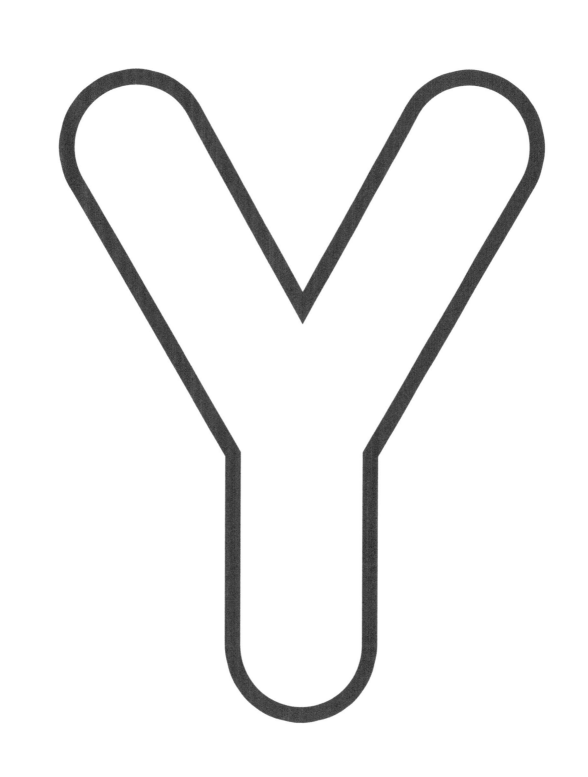

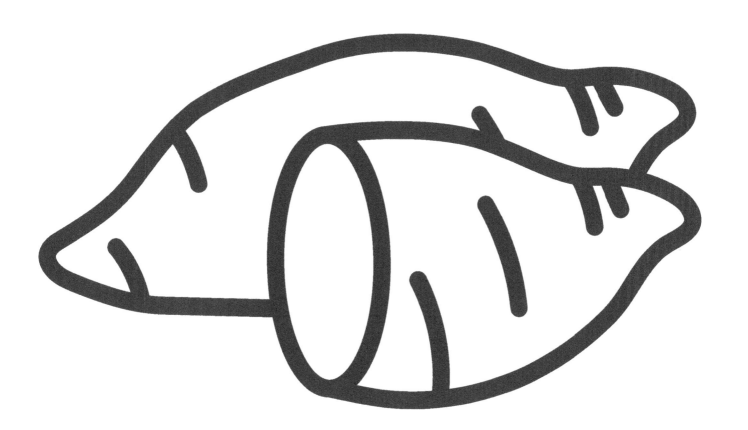

YAM

YO-YO

Z

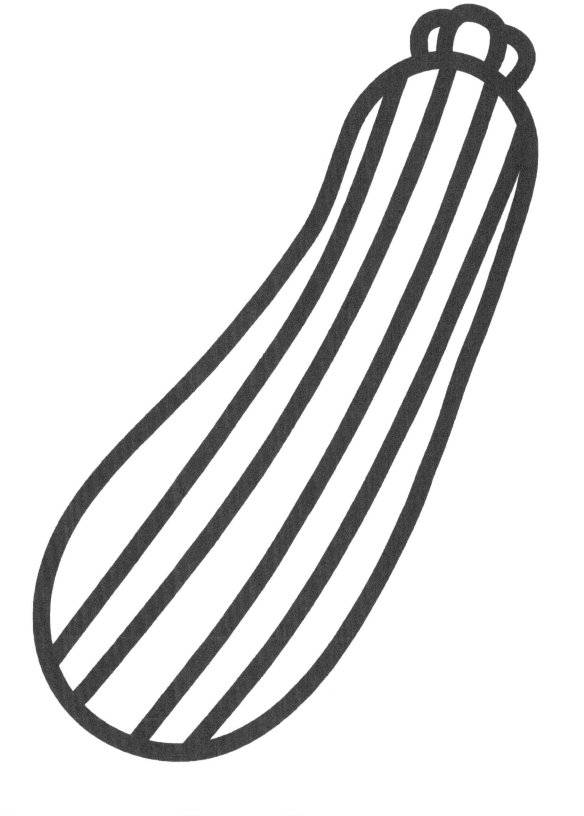

ZUCCHINI

ZEBRA

Made in the USA
Monee, IL
16 December 2024

74054083R00090